Kids' crafts

SOAPMAKING

LARK KIDS' CRAFTS

Kids' crafts

SOAPMAKING

50 Fun & Fabulous Soaps to Melt & Pour

Joe Rhatigan

LARK BOOKS
A Division of Sterling Publishing Co., Inc.
New York

Series Editor: JOE RHATIGAN
Art Director: CELIA NARANJO
Associate Editor: RAIN NEWCOMB
Photographer: STEVE MANN
Cover Designer: BARBARA ZARETSKY
Illustrations: CELIA NARANJO
Art Assistant: SHANNON YOKELEY
Art Intern: AVERY JOHNSON
Editorial Assistance: DELORES GOSNELL
Project Designers: TERRY TAYLOR &
                   ALLISON SMITH

Library of Congress Cataloging-in-Publication Data

Rhatigan, Joe.
  Soapmaking : 50 fun & fabulous soaps to melt & pour / Joe Rhatigan.
—1st ed.
       p. cm. — (Kids' crafts)
Includes index.
  ISBN 1-57990-416-5 (hard back)
  1. Soap. I. Title. II. Series.
  TP991.R48 2003
  668'.12—dc21

                                              2003000883

10 9 8 7 6 5 4 3 2 1

First Edition

Published by Lark Books, a division of
Sterling Publishing Co., Inc.
387 Park Avenue South, New York, N.Y. 10016

© 2003, Lark Books

Distributed in Canada by Sterling Publishing,
c/o Canadian Manda Group, One Atlantic Ave., Suite 105
Toronto, Ontario, Canada M6K 3E7

Distributed in the U.K. by Guild of Master Craftsman Publications Ltd., Castle
Place, 166 High Street, Lewes, East Sussex, England
BN7 1XU
Tel: (44) 1273 477374, Fax: (44) 1273 478606, Email: pubs thegmc-
group.com, Web: www.gmcpublications.com

Distributed in Australia by Capricorn Link (Australia) Pty Ltd.,
P.O. Box 704, Windsor, NSW 2756 Australia

The written instructions, photographs, designs, patterns, and projects in this
volume are intended for the personal use of the reader and may be repro-
duced for that purpose only. Any other use, especially commercial use, is for-
bidden under law without written permission of the copyright holder.

Every effort has been made to ensure that all the information in this book is
accurate. However, due to differing conditions, tools, and individual skills, the
publisher cannot be responsible for any injuries, losses, and other damages
that may result from the use of the information in this book.

If you have questions or comments about this book, please contact:
Lark Books
67 Broadway
Asheville, NC 28801
(828) 253-0467
Printed in Hong Kong

ISBN 1-57990-416-5

Acknowledgments

The following folks were essential ingredients for this book: Rain Newcomb, for her ability to dive in and make soap; Terry Taylor and Allison Smith, for their wonderful projects and bubbly personalities; Celia Naranjo for her sudsational design; Steve Mann, for his purty pictures; Brittany Jencks, for her inspiring soap business article; Shannon and Sally Yokeley, for providing our dog model; and moms Tana Jencks, Brenda Hill, Leslie Humphrey, Beverly Peterson, Allison Smith, and Deborah Morgenthal.

Thank you models: Devon Dickerson, Jake Hill, Nick Hill, Mimi Hill, Ingrid Humphrey, Eva Humphrey, Corrina Matthews, Larry Peterson, Ray Peterson, Jazzman Peterson, and especially, Dixie the dog.

Finally, I'd like to thank Thomas Yaley, Jr. at Yaley Enterprises (www.yaley.com) and Carole Krinskey at Life of the Party (www.soapplace.com) for supplying the materials for all the soaps in this book. We loved working with all these wonderful products.

Contents

Soaps, Suds, and Such

You're a long way from that little kid who refused to take a bath...

and hopefully nobody has had to threaten to wash your mouth out with soap in quite some time. But, I bet that in your mind, soap still suffers from a bad reputation. Or, if you don't have horrible soap memories, you may think of it as just plain boring. I mean, what is soap anyway but a block of white stuff used to get dirt off you, right?

Well...if you've skimmed through the pages of this book, then you already know what I'm about to say. If not, here it is: Not only can soap be great, big, and wonderful and come in all sorts of shapes, sizes, colors, and scents, but (and here's the part that I think will be surprising) you (yes, plain old you) can make awesome, awe-inspiring soap quickly and easily. You don't need to buy a bunch of tools, and you can start as soon as you get your hands on a block of soap base (easy to find at any craft store), a mold, a microwave oven, a spoon, and a measuring cup. And in mere minutes you'll be creating beautiful soaps, wacky soaps, useful soaps, or healthful soaps. You'll be making soaps to celebrate the seasons or the holidays, soaps for Grandma, Dad, your kid sister, and even your dog. Soap in the shape of a pizza!? Sure, why not? Eyeball soap!? Every home should have a pair.

What else is so cool about soapmaking?

• You don't have to be particularly patient. Once your soap is hardened, you can use it right away.

• It's hard to mess up your projects. And if you feel like you have, simply remelt and try again.

• You can work in the kitchen, and it's easy to clean up afterward. (Hey, it's soap!)

• Since the process is so easy, you'll find yourself experimenting with all sorts of creative soapmaking ideas quickly—perhaps as soon as you make your first soap.

• You can even set up a business and sell your soap.

• And, finally, even if the soap you make isn't exactly what you wanted, it's still useful.

What else will you need? Just this book. It will give you all the information you need to instantly start making soaps that will astound, thrill, and yes, even clean. All you need to do is keep reading. Have fun!

Start Here!

Many of the supplies you need for melt and pour soapmaking can be found around the house. Here's everything you need to start making great soaps.

SOAP BASE

Traditional soapmaking can be a tricky process, but with melt and pour soapmaking, the hard work has already been done for you. All you have to do is get to a craft store and buy your soap base.

Most soap bases come in blocks or bars, and they're usually clear or opaque (white), although there are also tons of precolored soap bases available. These are glycerin soaps (see page 11) that you can use right out of the package if you

Many melt and pour soap companies make soap curls, shavings, noodles, shapes, sheets, and more.

want to. Some bases also come with additives in them such as avocado, cucumber, vitamin E, and other good stuff for your skin.

Keep unused base wrapped in plastic to preserve moisture.

Buying Your Soap Base

• If you want to make soap you can see through, you'll want to buy a clear soap base.
• If you want to make white or pastel-colored soaps you can't see through, buy opaque (white) base.
• Decide how many soaps you want to make before you go shopping. You can usually make anywhere from three to six bars of soap per pound of base you buy, depending on how big your molds are.
• If you start melting and pouring soap, and you notice that your soap base smells funny, doesn't melt easily or pour smoothly, and doesn't lather well, consider buying a different brand of soap next time.

You've Got Glycerin in You!

Glycerin is a thick, colorless, slightly sweet liquid that is found in animal and vegetable fats. It has all sorts of uses besides just making soap. Glycerin is used to make dynamite and lubricate hydraulic jacks. It's also put into lotions, cosmetics, and ink. You even eat a lot of glycerin. It's used as a sugar substitute in many foods. It's also used to can fruit (such as jams and jellies), to keep the sugar in candy from crystallizing, and to hold the air in ice cream.

MOLDS

Right next to the soap bases in the craft store you should find the soap molds. But don't think you have to stick to using only them. You can also use candy molds, rubber molds, ice cube trays, PVC pipe pieces, potato chip containers, plastic food containers (microwave safe), plastic packaging, and other flexible containers you can find in your kitchen, basement, or garage. You can even create molds from aluminum foil. Try to avoid working with glass and metal molds. It's usually hard to get the soaps out of them.

Choosing Your Mold

Deciding what mold you'll use is the first step in creating your soap. Do you want to make one bar of soap or create a whole loaf that you can slice into a bunch of bars? Do you want a simple-looking soap, or something a little more snazzy?

• If you decide to use a plastic mold you found, make sure to let the soap cool a bit before pouring it. If the mold is flimsy, the high heat of the soap will melt it.

• Make sure the mold is flexible, yet strong enough to hold the hot liquid soap without spilling.

• Choose a clear mold if you're making a layered soap or a soap with embeds in it. That way you can see what you're doing.

Clockwise from top: a tray mold, a rubber mold, a single plastic mold, and a sand toy mold

With 3-D molds you can create cool 3-D soap shapes such as balls, eggs, shell shapes, and more. Simply close the mold and pour the soap in the top where the openings are. Use a funnel to keep from spilling soap.

Just a few of the items you can find in the kitchen that make good molds

• If you want to make a soap loaf, you can buy a loaf mold at a craft store or use a loaf pan with a piece of plastic wrap covering the inside of the pan.

• Explore the different soap molds available. There are deep molds, shallow molds, embossed molds, lollipop molds, and even massage soap molds with raised balls on one side for rubbing sore muscles.

OTHER STUFF

The rest of the tools you'll need may be right there in your kitchen. Get a parent's permission before using this stuff, and make sure you clean up when you're done. The following list outlines the tools and supplies you should have before you start a project.

Microwave Oven

A microwave oven is the best way to melt your soap base. Every make and model of microwave is different, so you'll need to experiment with yours to find out how your soap base reacts to its settings.

Microwave-Safe Measuring Cup

You can melt your soap base in any microwave-safe glass or

plastic container, though a measuring cup is great since it's easy to pour from, and you can measure exactly how much melted soap you used to fill certain molds. Glass containers can get very hot in the microwave, so use an oven mitt to remove them or try to use a plastic container. An even better bet is to follow the melting instructions on page 17.

Fragrance
If you want your soap to smell nice, you can purchase fragrance made especially for soap in the soap section of a craft supply store. For more on fragrances, see page 18.

Coloring
You can buy liquid or granular soap coloring in the soap section of a craft supply store. More on coloring on page 19.

Sharp Knife
The soap base is easy to cut with a sharp knife. It's like cutting a block of cheese. Don't use the big kitchen knife without a parent's permission first. Discuss with your parent whether or not he or she should do the cutting for you.

Cutting Board
Always cut your soap on a cutting board.

Cosmetic-Grade Sprayer Filled with Isopropyl (Rubbing) Alcohol
Most folks say that it's essential that you spray rubbing alcohol on any *embeds* (objects suspended in the soap) or layers of soaps before adding another layer. This prevents bubbles and helps the layers stick together. There are some soapmakers, however, who think that using alcohol is a waste of time. We suggest that you do use a spritz of alcohol between layers, but if you're uncomfortable with using rubbing alcohol, or if your parents think it's a bad idea, try your projects without using it, and see how it goes. You can use a plant sprayer, but you'll have better luck with a cosmetic-grade sprayer, which can be found in the cosmetics section of drugstores.

Vegetable Peeler or Butter Knife
Either of these tools is great for trimming soap edges, although rubbing the soap's edges with a towel also works.

Eyedropper
An eyedropper can be helpful if your liquid coloring comes in a bottle that doesn't have a spout at the end.

Wax Paper
If you put wax paper down on your work surface before you start, cleanup will be easier.

Large Craft Stick or Metal Spoon
You can use either of these items to mix color, fragrance, and other additives to your melted soap.

Soap Paints
Once your soaps are unmolded, you may want to add a little something extra to them. Use soap paints! They're made just for soaps, and they're easy to use. Look for them in the soap section of a craft supply store.

Toothpicks or Skewers
These can help you position any embeds in your soap.

Look at the project instructions for other tools or materials you might need.

Your Steps to Sud-sational Success

You've got your soap and tools, and you're all ready to go. Well, here are the steps you need to take. Each project in this book will have you following these steps more or less. Also in this section, you'll learn more about color, fragrance, and other things you can add to your soap.

1. Set Up Your Work Area

Your best bet is to set up shop in the kitchen. Make sure it's okay with Mom or Dad, and promise you'll clean up afterward.

• Get all of your supplies and tools out ahead of time.

2. Figure Out How Much Soap You Need

Most of the time you'll probably just guess how much you'll need. If you're a good guesser, go for it. Just remember that it's always better to overestimate than underestimate.

• If you like to know exactly how much soap you'll need, fill the mold with water and pour the water into a measuring cup. That's how much melted soap you'll need. Melt a little more soap than you need to make up for any soap that sticks to the sides of the measuring cup when you pour.

3. Cut the Soap

Cut the soap base into 1/2-inch cubes with the sharp knife. Put the cubes in the microwave-safe container.

4. Prepare the Mold

Apply a thin, even coat of petroleum jelly over the inside surface of the mold with a paper towel. You can also use a vegetable oil spray. Don't overspray—the mold only needs a very light touch of oil.

5. Melt the Soap

This is one of the most important steps as far as safety is concerned. The soap gets really hot, and you'll burn yourself if you're not careful here. Get a parent to help you out.

• Put the measuring cup in the microwave and heat on "high" for 20 seconds. Not any longer. Stir the soap with the craft stick or spoon.

• If the soap isn't melted completely, set the microwave for 10 more seconds. Check again, and stir. Heat again for five seconds if you have to. Don't let the soap boil.

• Here's a classic mistake: Whatever you do, don't put the microwave on for 20 minutes and think you'll just turn it off in 10 seconds. If you get called away or if you forget you're heating soap, you could have a horrible, hot mess and some pretty nasty soap on your hands.

• When the soap is melted, check to see if the container is hot. If it is, let it sit in the microwave until steam stops coming from the soap. For safety, wear an oven mitt to remove the measuring cup.

• If you overheat the soap, the base may turn amber and lose moisture, you may end up warping your mold, and any embedded objects may melt.

6. Add Fragrance

This soap smells okay without any fragrance added, though a little touch of juniper, pine, eucalyptus, fresh floral, citrus, bubblegum, or even strawberry shortcake really makes your soap special.

• There are two main types of oils you can buy for your soaps: essential oils, which are natural scents of flowers and herbs, and fragrance oils, which are synthetically produced scents. Fragrance oils are the better choice here for many reasons. First, you really need to know what you're doing with essential oils, and I don't recommend using them without a knowledgeable adult's supervision. Second, a great variety of fragrance oils is available along with fun combinations of smells. Finally, fragrance oils are a lot cheaper. Fragrance scents are also available next to the soap bases at craft stores.

• You can also use a favorite perfume or a little bit of shampoo, but don't use candle scents. In general, if the scent you want to use wasn't made for skin, don't use it.

• Scent should be added to your melted soap sparingly. After adding a few drops, mix slowly and sniff. If you don't smell anything, add more. Don't worry if your soap ends up smelling a little too strong. The smell will fade a bit.

• The amount you use depends on how strong the scent is, though as a general rule, you'll probably add only one to four drops of scent per ounce of melted soap.

• Too much scent will cloud the soap and irritate your skin.

• Scent your soap before coloring it since the scent may color the base. So if your scent turns your soap base a reddish color, and you add yellow, you may end up with a purplish soap instead of yellow.

7. Add Color

Use the coloring available in the soap section of the craft store. Don't use food coloring or coloring used for candles.

- If you're already using colored soap, you don't have to color it again!
- Add one to four drops of coloring per 4 ounces of soap. Mix gently but thoroughly after each drop added. If you use too much coloring, the soap may stain.
- If your soap begins to harden, reheat it for a few seconds.
- Coordinate your coloring with the fragrance. In other words, a black, citrus-smelling soap may confuse the senses, though a light orange citrus-smelling soap would be enjoyed. Here are some other hints:

- A soap with hot colors and a strong fragrance has an energizing effect, while a soap with cool colors and a refreshing scent is soothing.
- If you want to swirl two different colors, pour uncolored soap into your mold, add one drop of two different colors on opposite sides of the soap, and gently swirl the soap with a toothpick.
- Colored soap pieces embedded into your soap may run over time.

Cold
clean, refreshing

Cool
peaceful, calm, meditative

Warm
comforting

Hot
stimulating

Earthy, homey
grounding

Romantic
peaceful, soothing

This chart provides some guidelines on colors and the moods, emotions, and sensations they convey.

8. Pour the Soap into the Mold

Don't pour the soap while it's still steaming. You can even wait until a thin skin has formed on the top. Simply push it aside with a craft stick when you're ready to pour.

• Get the measuring cup as close to the mold as possible, and slowly pour the soap to the top of the mold.

9. Wait

• It can take anywhere from 20 minutes to an hour or more for your soap to set or harden.
• Test the soap by pressing lightly on the surface with your finger.

LOAF SOAPS

Loaf soaps are great when you want to make several bars of soap at once. A loaf mold is simply a bigger and longer mold. You'll usually need anywhere from 2 to 3 cups of melted soap to fill a loaf mold. Instead of buying a loaf mold, you can use a bread loaf pan. Before you pour soap into the pan, lay plastic wrap inside. This makes it easier to unmold the soap, though sometimes the wrinkles in the plastic wrap change the look of the soap.

Loaf inserts can be added to your loaf to give each bar you cut from it the same design.

10. Unmold

Make sure the soap is completely cool and hardened before trying to unmold it.

• Turn the mold upside down, and press gently on the bottom. The soap should pop right out. If it doesn't, wait for a half-hour and try again.

• Don't refrigerate your soaps to cool them off. If you're making a layered soap, the layers may separate.

• If you're still having trouble unmolding your soap, place the mold in a bowl of hot water. Make sure the soap doesn't get wet.

• Never use a knife or fork to try to remove the soap from the mold. You will probably mess up the soap, and you may lose a finger or two.

• Wrap the soap with clear plastic wrap to keep the soap from "sweating" until you're ready to use it.

• If you've poured a little bit too much soap into the mold, you'll end up with extra soap attached to it. Simply trim the soap with a butter or table knife. You can also use a paring knife or any knife that doesn't have a serrated edge.

OTHER THINGS TO ADD TO YOUR SOAP

Here's a short list of more stuff you can add to your soaps for some extra pizzazz.

Pearlescent powder: gives your soap an extra sparkle (available at craft stores in a variety of colors)

Cosmetic-grade glitter: available at body care stores and pharmacies with body care sections (don't use normal glitter)

Dried fruit

Crushed, dried flower petals

Herbs

11. Clean Up

Hand wash all of your tools and molds before putting them in the dishwasher. Soap residue can create a mess in the dishwasher if not removed first.

• That's it. You've got soap.

12. Wrap It Up

If you're not going to use your finished soap right away, wrap it in plastic wrap or store it in a see-through cellophane bag. Why?

• First, glycerin, the main ingredient in the soap, attracts moisture from the air, so if a glycerin-based soap is left out, beads of moisture will form on the bar, and the soap will look like it's sweating. This makes the soap feel slimy and look sort of yucky.

• Second, wrapping your soap preserves the strength of the fragrance you may have added.

• Finally, it looks cool. Once you wrap your soap in plastic, you can then cover it in interesting paper, ribbons, strings, and more. You can attach seashells to an ocean-themed bar, or simply adhere a piece of paper on the back of the wrapped soap with the ingredients listed and who created the soap.

yikes!
she's got soap!

The Projects

Here they are! More than 50 awesome projects to shift your soapmaking imagination into high gear. Experiment with additives, fragrances, colors, molds, soap bases, and more.

Supplies

You'll need these supplies for each of the projects in this book. Refer to it before beginning each project.

- Opaque or clear soap base
- Mold
- Wax paper for your work surface
- Petroleum jelly or cooking spray to prepare the mold
- Sharp knife
- Cutting board
- Measuring cup or other microwave-safe container
- Microwave oven
- Large craft stick or spoon to stir melted soaps
- Eyedropper for adding color
- Butter knife to trim completed soaps

Final Notes

You can replace clear or opaque soaps in the instructions with precolored soaps, which are also available at craft stores. It saves you the step of having to color the soap.

Read through the instructions before starting a project. This will give you the chance to decide whether or not you want to use all the materials (additives, colors, fragrances) listed.

One of the best things about creating with soap is how quickly you get good at it. After doing a soap or two you're ready for more techniques.

Dog's Best Friend

Your dog's skin will appreciate a bath with this chemical-free soap, even if your dog doesn't.

WHAT YOU NEED

Soap: opaque soap base
Mold: embossed dog bone mold
Supplies on page 23
Measuring spoons
Tea tree essential oil
Cedar essential oil
Castor oil
Color of choice
Rubbing alcohol and sprayer

Though perfect for dogs, never use this soap with cats.

WHAT YOU DO

1 Prepare the mold, and cut and melt the soap base.

2 Let the soap cool for three to five minutes, or until it stops steaming. Carefully pour the melted base into the raised (the bone) section of the mold. Stop when you get to the top of the bone.

3 Remelt the remaining opaque soap in the measuring cup, and add 1 teaspoon each of tea tree oil, cedar oil, and castor oil. The tea tree and cedar oils are good for the dog's skin, and the castor oil keeps your dog's fur shiny and soft. Mix slowly.

4 Add any coloring you may want, and mix again.

5 Make sure the dog bone soap has a skin on it. The skin should be thick enough to hold the weight of the next layer of soap.

6 Make sure the melted soap is not steaming before continuing with this step. Spray the top of the hardened soap with a light layer of rubbing alcohol, and pour the colored soap into the mold.

7 Let the soap harden completely before removing it from the mold.

8 Try, just try, to get your dog in the bathtub!

Dirty Little Brother Soap

An embedded soap has some sort of object in it, from a small toy, a coin, or even another piece of soap. The only way your dirty brother can get to the really cool toy is by using up all the soap.

What else can you imagine embedding in soap?

WHAT YOU NEED

Soap: clear soap base
Mold: rectangular loaf mold
Supplies on page 23
Plastic trucks or other toys
Rubbing alcohol and sprayer
Fragrance of choice
Green coloring

WHAT YOU DO

1 Prepare the mold. Cut and melt enough clear soap to fill the bottom of the mold. Pour it into the mold.

2 Spray the trucks with the rubbing alcohol. Place them upside down in the layer of clear soap you just poured.

3 Cut and melt more clear soap. Add fragrance if you want, and stir the soap slowly.

4 Once a thin skin has formed on the layer of soap you poured, spritz the layer and trucks with rubbing alcohol, and pour the melted soap into the mold, stopping when you reach the bottom of the truck tires.

5 Cut and melt more clear soap. Add fragrance and green coloring. Stir them into the soap slowly.

6 Spray the setting soap with the rubbing alcohol. Pour the melted green soap into the mold.

7 Let the soap harden completely. Unmold the soap and cut it into slices. (Don't slice up the trucks!)

Multicolored Layer Soap

This fun technique can be used in any kind of mold you want. You can use two, three, or more colors.

WHAT YOU NEED

Soap: clear soap base
Mold: square or rectangular mold
Supplies on page 23
Fragrance of choice
Colors of choice
Rubbing alcohol and sprayer

Did you know that in the 16th century, people didn't think much of bathing? They believed that there was a layer of oil covering the skin that kept diseases from getting in.

They assumed bathing would strip away this layer, exposing them to illness and disease. Of course, not washing up was one of the things that made the plagues that swept through this time so devastating.

Benjamin Franklin was the proud owner of the very first bathtub in the American colonies.

6 Let a skin form on top of the first layer. The skin should be thick enough to hold the weight of the second layer. You can press down with your finger to check.

WHAT YOU DO

1 Prepare the mold. Cut and melt the soap base for the first layer. Since you'll be melting and pouring several times with this project, consider making more than one soap at a time.

2 Let the soap cool for three to five minutes, or until it stops steaming.

3 Add fragrance and one color. Mix together slowly.

4 Pour the first layer of soap into the bottom of the mold.

5 Cut and melt soap for the second layer. Add fragrance and a different color. Mix together slowly. Let it cool slightly.

7 Once a firm skin has formed on the first layer, spritz it with the rubbing alcohol, and immediately pour the second layer on top of the first layer. If the first layer isn't hard enough, the melted soap you pour on top of it will melt the layer.

Also, if the liquid soap you're pouring is too hot, that first layer will melt anyway.

8 Repeat steps 5 through 7 until you've filled the mold. Let the soap harden completely before unmolding.

Superstar

Give this soap to someone special— a real life superstar.

Soap: clear soap base

Mold: square or rectangular mold and star mold

Supplies on page 23

Fragrance of choice

Colors of choice

Rubbing alcohol and sprayer

Vegetable peeler

WHAT YOU DO

1. Create the ribbon curls by first making a multilayered soap (see page 28). Once the soap has hardened completely, unmold it, and use the vegetable peeler to shave the block into curls.

2. Put the curls in the freezer. This keeps them from melting when you pour hot soap over them.

3. Prepare the star-shaped mold. When the curls are very cold, place them loosely in the mold.

4. Cut and melt enough soap to fill the mold. Add fragrance if you want, but don't add any color. Stir the fragrance in slowly, and let the soap cool a bit.

5. Pour the soap into the mold. Let it harden completely before unmolding.

Sudsy Snapshot

Send your grandparents a picture of yourself embedded in soap.

 WHAT YOU DO

1 Copy the photograph you want to use onto a sheet of acetate. You can get this done cheaply at any copy center.

2 Prepare the mold. Cut the picture out of the acetate, leaving a ¼-inch margin around the edges. Set it aside.

3 Cut and melt a little bit of the clear soap. Pour it into the mold so that the melted soap just covers the bottom. Let it harden until a thick skin forms.

 WHAT YOU NEED

Soap: clear and opaque soap base
Mold: rectangular mold
Supplies on page 23
Photograph
Acetate*
Use of a color photocopier
Scissors
Rubbing alcohol and sprayer
Fragrance of choice
Cosmetic-grade glitter (optional)
* These clear, plastic sheets are available at paper supply stores or copy centers.

4 Spray the acetate photo with the rubbing alcohol. Place it face down in the soap mold.

5 Cut and melt the rest of the soap. Add fragrance.

6 Pour the soap into the mold, leaving a ¼-inch gap at the top. Let it harden until a thick skin forms.

7 Cut and melt a small amount of the opaque base. Spray the setting soap with the rubbing alcohol.

8 Pour a layer of opaque soap on top of the clear soap. Unmold the soap once it has completely hardened.

31

Have a Ball

Here are some great gift ideas for the sports fans in your home.

You can buy paints specifically made for soap decorating. It's fun painting the raised decorations of molded soaps. You may want to practice on paper first, and if you make a mistake on the soap, keep a damp rag nearby to wipe it off before trying again.

 ## WHAT YOU NEED

Soap: opaque soap base
Mold: football- or soccer-shaped molds
Supplies on page 23
Fragrance of choice
Brown coloring (for football)
Soap paints
Paintbrush

 ## WHAT YOU DO

1 Prepare the mold. Cut and melt the soap. Add fragrance and coloring, and stir the mixture slowly.

2 Pour the melted soap into the mold. Let it harden completely before unmolding.

3 Paint the details on the ball with the soap paints.

What a Gem!

Make a bunch of these gems, and surprise your family by placing them in a bowl next to the sink.

 WHAT YOU NEED

Soap: clear soap base
Mold: any mold at least 1½ inches deep
Supplies on page 23
Fragrance of choice
Coloring of choice
Butter, paring or any unserrated knife

 WHAT YOU DO

1 Prepare the mold. Cut and melt the soap. Add the fragrance and coloring. Stir them into the soap slowly.

2 Pour the melted soap into the mold. Let it harden before unmolding.

3 Cut the soap into small chunks. Cut facets in them to make them look like gems.

Put the soap gems in a treasure chest. Hide it. Present your friend with a map and make him or her find the soap.

33

Travel Soap

Give this soap to someone about to embark on a vacation.

WHAT YOU NEED

Soap: clear and opaque soap base
Mold: rectangular loaf mold
Supplies on page 23
Cheese grater
Small toy airplanes
Rubbing alcohol and sprayer
Fragrance of choice
Blue coloring

Did you know the ancient Greeks didn't use soap? They lathered up with sand instead! Then they rubbed on some oil and scraped it off with a flat instrument that looked like a comb, called a *strigil*.

WHAT YOU DO

1. Grate some opaque soap base with the cheese grater. Mush the pieces together into cloud-shaped forms and set the clouds aside.

2. Prepare the mold. Cut and melt enough soap to fill the bottom of the mold. Pour it into the mold.

3. Spritz the plastic airplanes with the rubbing alcohol, and place them upside down in the layer of clear soap you just poured.

4. Once a firm skin has formed on the layer of poured soap, place the clouds you made in step 1 on top of each airplane. If you're sinking the airplanes further into the soap, wait until the soap hardens a little longer.

5. Cut and melt the rest of the soap. Add fragrance and a small amount of the blue coloring. If you put too much coloring in, you won't be able to see the planes.

6. Spritz the poured layer of soap with the alcohol, and immediately pour the melted soap into the mold.

Funky swirls

Did you know the ancient Egyptians mostly used soap for treating icky skin problems instead of taking baths?

Adding color to opaque soap creates fun pastels.

WHAT YOU NEED

Soap: opaque soap base

Mold: potato chip can

Supplies on page 23

Hand towels or something to prop up the mold

Fragrance of choice

Colors of choice

1 Put the chip can on top of the towels at an angle. Make sure it isn't going to roll away from you.

2 Cut and melt the soap. Add the fragrance and one of the colors. Stir the mixture slowly.

3 Let the soap cool a bit, and pour the melted soap into the can.

4 Once a firm skin forms on the soap you just poured, move the can so that it lays at a different angle on top of the towels.

5 Cut and melt more soap. Add fragrance and a different color. Stir the mixture slowly.

6 Let the soap cool slightly, then pour it into the can.

7 Repeat steps 4 through 6 until you've filled the can. Let the soap harden completely.

8 Peel away the can, and slice the soap.

Did you know the trade of soapmaking started up in Europe? Soap was made up mostly of oil from olive trees. The business became so popular that in 1622, King James I of England paid his best soapmaker $100,000 a year!

FOR THE HOLIDAYS

Bring a little cheer into your home with these festive soaps.

New Year's Confetti

Your New Year's resolution: Save all your soapmaking scraps to turn into this soap.

WHAT YOU NEED

Soap: opaque soap base and colored soap scraps (shavings, curlicues, chunks)

Mold: loaf mold

Supplies on page 23

Fragrance of choice

 WHAT YOU DO

1 Prepare the loaf mold. Loosely place the colored soap scraps in the mold so there's room between the pieces for melted soap.

2 Cut and melt the soap base. Add fragrance and mix it in slowly.

3 Pour the melted soap into the mold. Let it harden completely.

4 Remove the soap from the mold, and slice it into bars.

Did you know in the third century, Rome had 11 public baths? The Baths of Caracalla could cater to up to 1,600 people at a time.

You can also do this project by following the multilayered soap instructions on page 28. Simply add soap scraps to each layer of soap you pour into the mold.

39

Be My Valentine

Make one for all of your friends.

 WHAT YOU NEED

Soap: clear soap base
Mold: small heart-shaped mold
Supplies on page 23
Fragrance of choice
Pink coloring
Cosmetic-grade glitter (optional)
Plastic bracelet
Tape

 **WHAT YOU DO**

1 Prepare the mold. Cut and melt the soap. Add fragrance, coloring, and glitter. Stir them into the soap slowly.

2 Pour the melted soap into the mold.

3 Take the bracelet and carefully place the middle of it into the melted soap. Use the tape to hold the bracelet in place.

4 Let the soap harden. Then remove it from the mold.

Hearts in the Right Place

Make this scent-sational loaf to share
with your loved ones.

 WHAT YOU NEED

Soap: clear soap base and 2 heart-shaped
soap inserts
Mold: rectangular loaf mold
Supplies on page 23
Fragrance of choice
Pink or red coloring
Cosmetic-grade glitter
Rubbing alcohol and sprayer

WHAT YOU DO

1 Prepare the loaf mold. Cut and melt the soap. Add fragrance, a small amount of pink or red coloring, and glitter. Mix them together slowly. Make sure the soap is a lighter color than the hearts.

2 Pour about ¼ inch of soap into the loaf mold.

3 Spray the heart-shaped inserts with rubbing alcohol, and set them on top of the soap you just poured.

4 Pour the rest of the melted soap into the loaf mold.

5 When the soap is hard, take it out of the mold. Cut the loaf into bars.

Easter Eggs

This soap is truly egg-cellent.

Put embeds in the middle of your soap for extra fun. Nobody will know what's in them if you use opaque soap!

 WHAT YOU NEED

Soap: opaque soap base
Mold: egg-shaped 3-D mold (see page 13)
Supplies on page 23
Fragrance of choice
Coloring of choice
Soap paints
Paintbrush

 **WHAT YOU DO**

 Prepare the mold. Cut and melt the soap base. Add fragrance and coloring. Mix them into the soap slowly.

2 Pour the soap into the mold. Let it harden completely.

3 Take the soap out of the mold, and paint designs on the soap.

If you're giving this soap away as a gift, make 12 of them and place them in a used egg carton.

April Fool's Soap

It looks like candy. It smells like oranges. It's actually soap.

 WHAT YOU NEED

Soap: opaque soap base

Mold: disk-shaped mold

Supplies on page 23

Citrus fragrance

Red soap paint

Paintbrush

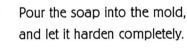 WHAT YOU DO

1 Prepare the mold. Cut and melt the soap. Add the citrus fragrance and stir it in.

2 Pour the soap into the mold, and let it harden completely.

3 Remove the soap from the mold, and place it right-side up on your work surface.

4 Paint red peppermint swirls on the surface of the soap.

5 Wrap it up and give it to someone for April Fool's Day.

Halloween Treats

Wrap up these cute Halloween treats.
Just make sure nobody tries to eat them.

WHAT YOU NEED

Soap: opaque soap base

Mold: square or rectangular loaf mold

Supplies on page 23

Fragrance of choice

Orange and yellow coloring

Rubbing alcohol and sprayer

Butter or paring knife

WHAT YOU DO

1 Prepare the loaf mold. Cut and melt the opaque soap for the first layer. Add fragrance—but no coloring—and mix slowly. Pour the mold one-third full.

2 Remelt the soap in your measuring cup. Add orange coloring, and mix it into the soap slowly.

3 Let the melted soap cool slightly. Once the first layer has a firm skin on it, spray it with rubbing alcohol. Immediately pour the melted soap into the mold.

4 Cut and melt soap for the final layer. Add fragrance and yellow coloring. Mix them into the soap slowly.

5 Let the melted soap cool slightly. Once the second layer has a firm skin on it, spray it with rubbing alcohol.

6 Pour the melted soap into the mold. Let the soap harden completely.

7 Unmold the soap, and cut it into wedge shapes. Round the edges with a knife if you want.

Snowmen

Let it snow! Let it snow! Let it snow!

WHAT YOU NEED

Soap: opaque soap base
Mold: snowman mold
Supplies on page 23
Fragrance of choice
Cosmetic-grade glitter
Soap paint
Paintbrush

WHAT YOU DO

1 Prepare the mold. Cut and melt the soap. Add fragrance and glitter. Mix them into the soap slowly.

2 Pour the melted soap into the mold. Let it harden completely.

3 Remove the soap from the mold. Paint the details onto the snowman with the soap paint.

Winter  Wonderland

Snow globe soaps are easy to make, and they look great anywhere.

WHAT YOU NEED

Soap: clear and opaque soap base

Mold: snow globe mold*

Supplies on page 23

Snow globe embed*

* Available at craft stores or in snow globe soap kits

WHAT YOU DO

1. Prepare the mold. Cut and melt the clear soap.

2. Pour a small amount of the soap into the mold.

The deep snow globe mold is great for embedding marbles, small balls, and small plastic toys.

3 Carefully place the snow globe into the layer of soap you just poured.

4 Pour the rest of the melted soap on top of the snow globe, leaving about $\frac{1}{4}$ inch of space at the top of the mold.

5 Cut and melt the opaque soap. Let it cool slightly, then, once a thin skin has formed on the layer you already poured, fill the top of the mold with the opaque soap.

6 After the soap has hardened completely, remove it from the mold.

47

Gross Eyeballs

This soap is perfect anytime you want to have a little scare. Leave one in the soap dish, and wait for the screaming to begin.

WHAT YOU NEED

Soap: opaque soap base

Mold: circular 3-D mold
(see page 13)

Soap paint

Paintbrush

WHAT YOU DO

1 Prepare the mold. Cut and melt the soap. Add fragrance. Stir the mixture slowly.

2 Pour the melted soap into the 3-D mold. Let the soap harden completely before unmmolding.

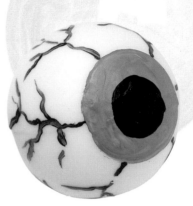

3 Paint on the pupil, iris, and blood vessels with the soap paints.

If you only have a half-round mold, you can still do this project. Pour one half of the soap, and unmold it. Pour the second half of the soap, and as it cools, gently place the first half on top of it. Voilà, you've got an eyeball.

Hand Soap

The next time someone asks you to give him a hand, give him one of these.

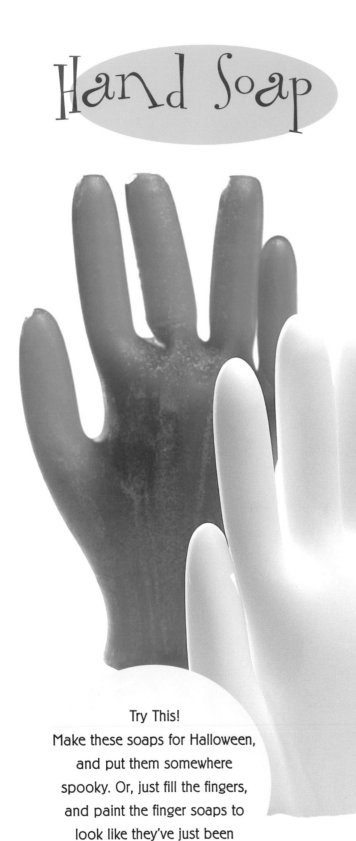

Try This!
Make these soaps for Halloween, and put them somewhere spooky. Or, just fill the fingers, and paint the finger soaps to look like they've just been chopped off. Yuck.

WHAT YOU NEED

Soap: opaque soap base
Mold: latex glove
Supplies on page 23
2-liter soda bottle
Scissors
Rubber bands
Fragrance of choice
Coloring of choice

WHAT YOU DO

1 Carefully cut the top off the soda bottle.
Prepare the mold by putting the latex glove
inside the bottle. Wrap the opening of the glove
around the opening of the container. Use the rubber bands to hold it in place. Make sure that no part
of the glove is lying on the bottom of the bottle.

2 Cut and melt the soap. Add
fragrance and coloring. Stir
them into the soap slowly.

3 Let the soap cool for up to five minutes,
or until steam stops rising from it. Slowly
pour the soap into the glove.

4 Once the soap is hard,
remove the glove from
the container, and gently
peel it off the hand soap.

51

Alphabet Soap

Making these soaps
is as easy as A B C.

Soap: clear soap base
Mold: letter molds
Supplies on page 23
Fragrances of choice
Colors of choice

 WHAT YOU DO

1 Prepare the molds. Cut and melt the soap. Add fragrance and coloring. Stir them into the soap slowly.

2 Pour the melted soap into some of the molds. Let the soaps harden.

3 Unmold, and repeat with other letters, colors, and fragrances until you have enough to write some sudsy poetry.

Try this!
For a special present, make all the letters to write a message to one of your friends. Wrap up the letters in random order and see if your friend can unscramble the message.

53

All Smiles

Need a smile? Make this soap, and put on a happy face.

WHAT YOU NEED

Soap: opaque soap base
Mold: circular 3-D mold (see page 13)
Supplies on page 23
Fragrance of choice
Coloring of choice
Soap paint
Paintbrush

WHAT YOU DO

1 Prepare the mold. Cut and melt the soap. Add fragrance and coloring. Stir them into the soap slowly.

2 Pour the melted soap into the mold. Let it harden.

3 Unmold it, and paint on some simple faces.

Try this!
Make different faces on
each soap, and each day,
use the soap that matches
your mood.

54

Soap in a Loaf

You can recycle leftover chunks of soap for this project, or make new ones.

Try this!
Use the alphabet letters on page 52, or pour melted opaque soap into the loaf mold for a stained-glass effect.

 WHAT YOU NEED

Soap: clear soap base
Mold: loaf mold and a bar soap mold
Supplies on page 23
Fragrance of choice
Colors of choice
Rubbing alcohol and sprayer

 WHAT YOU DO

1 Create three or four bars of soap. Use a different color for each soap.

2 Cut the hardened soaps into chunks, and place them in the freezer.

3 Prepare the loaf mold. Cut and melt soap to fill the mold. Add fragrance. Let the soap cool slightly.

4 Place the cold chunks of soap in the mold.

5 Spray the chunks with the rubbing alcohol, and then pour the melted soap into the loaf mold. Let the soap harden. Unmold it, and slice it into bars.

55

Googly Eyes Massage Bar

With this soap, all eyes will be on you.

 WHAT YOU NEED

Soap: clear and opaque soap base

Mold: massage bar mold*

Supplies on page 23

Plastic wiggly eyes

Rubbing alcohol and sprayer

Toothpick

Fragrance of choice

Coloring of choice

* This mold has raised (embossed) balls on the bottom.

1 Prepare the mold. Cut and melt enough clear soap to fill the holes in the bottom of the massage bar mold. Pour the soap into the holes.

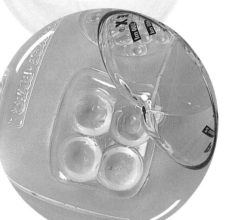

2 Spray the wiggly eyes with the rubbing alcohol. Place them upside down in the soap-filled holes of the mold before the soap has had time to harden. Use the toothpick to help position the eyes.

3 Cut and melt the opaque or clear soap. (You can use either.) Add fragrance and coloring. Stir them into the soap slowly.

4 Once a firm skin has formed on the layer you poured, spray it with the rubbing alcohol. Pour the melted soap into the mold.

5 Let the soap harden before unmolding.

It's Springtime!

Decals are an attractive and easy way to decorate your soap.

 WHAT YOU NEED

Soap: clear soap base

Mold: any molds you want

Supplies on page 23

Spring-themed decals made especially for soap*

Scissors

Fragrance of choice

Coloring of choice

Cosmetic-grade glitter

* Available in the soap section of your craft store.

WHAT YOU DO

1 Cut out the decals, leaving a ¼-inch margin around the edge. Cut and melt the soap. Add fragrance, coloring, and glitter. Once you've poured the soap and let it harden, unmold it and place it right-side up on your work surface.

2 Put a decal in warm water for 30 seconds. Dip your finger in the water, and wet the soap where you'll put the decal.

3 Take the decal out of the water, and with the paper backing still attached, place it on the soap. Lightly hold one edge of the decal in place and slide the paper backing out from under the decal. Gently adjust the decal and smooth out any wrinkles or air bubbles with your finger. Soap decals will last as long as your soap does.

Butterfly Flutterby

Welcome the end of cold, nasty weather with these bright and colorful soaps.

Try this!
Get a book on butterflies from the library. How many different kinds can you make out of soap?

 WHAT YOU NEED

Soap: opaque soap base
Mold: butterfly-shaped mold
Supplies on page 23
Fragrance of choice
Coloring of choice
Cosmetic-grade glitter
Soap paint
Paintbrush

WHAT YOU DO

1 Prepare the mold. Cut and melt the soap. Add fragrance, color, and glitter. Mix the soap slowly.

2 Pour the soap into the mold. Let it harden.

3 After the soap is hard, take it out of the mold.

4 Paint some colors onto the details on the top of the soap with the soap paint.

Bug Off

These little soaps have a powerful scent to keep summer's bugs away.

WHAT YOU NEED

Soap: opaque soap base

Mold: mold with embossed bug shape on top

Supplies on page 23

Citronella fragrance

Coloring of choice

Cosmetic-grade glitter

Rubbing alcohol and sprayer

Soap paint

Paintbrush

 **WHAT YOU DO**

1 Prepare the mold. Cut and melt soap for the bug shape of the mold. Add the citronella, color, and glitter. Stir the mixture slowly.

2 Pour the melted soap into the mold, filling just the bug shape.

3 Cut and melt soap for the rest of the mold. Add citronella and coloring. Stir the mixture slowly.

4 Once a thin skin has formed on the soap you poured, spray it with the rubbing alcohol. The skin should be thick enough to hold the weight of the second layer. You can press down with your finger to check.

5 Let the melted soap cool slightly. Then pour it on top of the first layer of soap.

6 Let the soap harden and unmold it. Highlight parts of the bugs with paint if you like.

LoVely Little Ladybugs

Ladybugs are good at cleaning pests off plants. (They eat them!)
Let these cool critters clean the dirt off you.

 WHAT YOU NEED

Soap: clear soap base
Mold: ladybug-shaped mold
Supplies on page 23
Fragrance of choice
Red coloring
Black soap paint
Paintbrush

 WHAT YOU DO

1 Prepare the mold. Cut and melt the soap. Add fragrance and red coloring. Stir them slowly into the melted soap.

2 Pour the soap into the mold. Let it harden.

3 Unmold the soap and place it right-side up on your work surface.

4 Paint the spots and eyes of the ladybug.

Did you know in 1399, England's King Henry IV instituted the Order of the Bath, which ordered his knights to take a bath at least once in their lives?

Autumn Colors

You'll really fall for these soaps.

WHAT YOU NEED

Soap: opaque soap base
Mold: leaf- and acorn-shaped molds
Supplies on page 23
Fragrance of choice
Fall colors
Cosmetic-grade glitter

WHAT YOU DO

1 Prepare the molds. Cut and melt the soap. Add fragrance, coloring, and glitter. Stir them into the soap slowly.

2 Pour the soap into the molds. Let the soaps harden completely.

3 Unmold the soaps, and repeat with different colors and fragrances if you want.

Frosty the Soapman

You don't need snow to make this guy.

 WHAT YOU NEED

Soap: opaque soap base and scrap piece of orange

Mold: suitable mold for hat

Supplies on page 23

Small glass bowl

Measuring spoons

1½ tablespoons liquid glycerin*

1 heaping tablespoon cornstarch, plus more for sprinkling

Fragrance of choice

Wax paper

Wooden skewer

Soap paints

Paintbrush

Toothpick

Black coloring

Twigs for arms

* Available at pharmacies and some craft stores

WHAT YOU DO

1. In the small glass bowl, mix together the liquid glycerin, cornstarch, and fragrance. Sprinkle a sheet of wax paper with some more cornstarch. Set it aside.

Try this! Make a snowman that looks like he's melting.

2 Cut and melt the soap, and pour it into the glass bowl. Stir the melted soap into the mixture. When the soap starts to harden and cool off, put it on the sheet of wax paper.

3 Coat your hands with cornstarch, and knead the soap until it's smooth.

4 Make the soap into three balls of different sizes. Stack them on top of each other. Push the wooden skewer through the middle of the soaps to hold them in place. Leave about ¼ inch of the skewer sticking out of the top of the head.

5 Paint the snowman's nose, eyes, and buttons with the soap paint. Mold a small piece of the orange soap into a nose. Put it on the snowman's face with the toothpick.

6 Prepare the mold for the hat. Cut and melt more opaque soap. Add fragrance and black coloring. Pour the melted soap into the mold.

7 Place the hat on the tip of the skewer. Stick the twigs into the side of the snowman's body.

SoapoSaurus

For a roaring good bath, create these litle dinos on a rope.

WHAT YOU NEED

Soap: clear soap base

Mold: dinosaur-shaped mold

Supplies on page 23

2- to 3- foot-long piece of ribbon or string

Tape

Fragrance of choice

Coloring of choice

Cosmetic-grade glitter

WHAT YOU DO

1 Prepare the mold. Fold the ribbon or string in half. Stick the ends in the mold, and tape the ribbon in place on the outside of the mold. (See pages 96 and 97 for more information on this technique.)

2 Cut and melt the soap. Add fragrance, coloring, and glitter. Stir them into the soap slowly.

3 Pour the melted soap into the mold. Let it harden. Unmold the soap.

Fossils

Use toy bugs or shells to make quite an impression on this soap.

 **WHAT YOU NEED**

Soap: opaque soap base
Mold: any mold you want
Supplies on page 23
Fragrance of choice
Brown and black coloring
Toothpick
Plastic bugs, flowers, shells, etc.

WHAT YOU DO

1 Prepare the mold. Cut and melt the soap. Add fragrance and brown coloring. Stir them into the soap slowly.

2 Pour the melted soap into the mold. Add a few drops of black coloring, and swirl it in with the toothpick.

3 Let the soap harden slightly. Push the plastic bugs, flowers, shells, or whatever into the soap. Make sure to push them in upside down.

4 Let the soap harden. Pull the plastic bugs out of the soap. Use the toothpick to help pry them out. Unmold the soap.

Leapin' Lizards

Who says cookie cutters are only for cookies?
They're great for soap, too!

 WHAT YOU NEED

Soap: opaque soap base

Mold: cookie sheet

Supplies on page 23

Aluminum foil

Fragrance of choice

Green coloring

Lizard-shaped cookie cutter (Any cookie cutter will do!)

Soap paints

Paintbrush

1 Line the cookie sheet with the aluminum foil.

2 Cut and melt the soap. Add fragrance and coloring. Stir them into the soap slowly.

Did you know that a workman who left the soap mixing machine on too long was responsible for making Ivory Soap float? He poured the soap instead of throwing it out. A few weeks later, letters began arriving asking for more soap that floated. Enough air had been worked into the soap mixture that the soap floated, and a legend was born.

3 Pour a ½-inch-thick layer of melted soap into the box you made in step 1. Pour slowly to make sure your aluminum mold doesn't spring a leak.

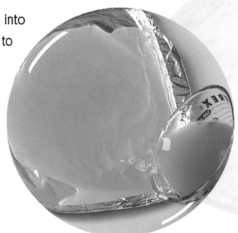

4 Let the soap harden slightly before removing it from the aluminum box.

5 Cut the lizard out of the soap with the cookie cutter. Paint the soap if you want.

Did you know the Lever brothers, who created Lifebuoy soap in 1895, were the first to come up with the term "B.O." for body odor?

Froggy Friend

This amphibian is so cute, you'll want to keep making more and more...until you croak.
(Ouch! Bad joke.)

 WHAT YOU NEED

Soap: clear and opaque soap base
Molds: frog mold and a flat round mold
Supplies on page 23
Wiggly eyes
Toothpick
Fragrance of choice
Green coloring
Rubbing alcohol and sprayer
Scissors
Bug decals*

* See page 58 for more information on decals.

 WHAT YOU DO

1 Prepare the frog mold. Cut and melt the clear soap. Pour a tiny amount into the eye spaces of the frog mold.

2 Put the wiggly eyes into the frog's eyes. Use the toothpick to help position the eyes.

3   Add fragrance and green coloring to the rest of the melted
    soap. Remelt if you have to. Mix the soap together slowly.

4   Once the eyes have a thin skin on them, spray
    the eye areas with the rubbing alcohol.
    Immediately pour the melted soap into the
    frog mold.

5   Prepare the flat round mold. Cut and melt
    the opaque soap. Add fragrance and
    green coloring. Pour the soap into the
    mold. Let it form a skin on top.

6   Pierce the skin with a toothpick. Liquid
    soap will well up on top of the skin.
    Gently place the frog on top of the liquid
    soap. Let it harden completely before
    unmolding. Add decals in you want.

Tidal Pool

Create a good home for some soapy sea critters.

 WHAT YOU NEED

Soap: clear or opaque soap base

Molds: sea creature molds and a round pan

Supplies on page 23

Fragrance of choice

Colors of choice

Aluminum foil

Cornmeal

WHAT YOU DO

1   Cut and melt the soap for the first sea creature. You can make them out of clear or opaque soap. Add the fragrance and coloring you want. Stir them into the soap slowly.

2   Create several sea creature soaps. Use different colors for each one. Place the critters in the freezer until you need them.

3   Line the round pan with the aluminum foil. Sprinkle the bottom with cornmeal to make sand.

4   Cut and melt clear soap. Add fragrance and a little bit of coloring if you like. Stir them in slowly.

5   Arrange the sea creatures in the pan.

6   Let the soap mixture cool slightly, then pour it into the pan). Let the soap harden, then take it out of the pan.

Queen Isabel of Spain boasted that she only bathed twice in her life— once when she was born and once before she was married.

73

Hold the Pickles

Make some fries and a large cola to supersize this soap.

What other kinds of food can you make? What scent do you think this soap should have?

WHAT YOU NEED

Soap: opaque soap base

Molds: round mold and a dome-shaped mold

Supplies on page 23

Aluminum foil

Fragrance of choice

Green, yellow, brown, and red coloring

Butter knife

PVC pipe

Decorative toothpick

Soap paints

Paintbrush

WHAT YOU DO

1 Cut and melt a small amount of the soap. Add fragrance and some green coloring for the lettuce.

2 Slowly pour a thin layer of soap onto a sheet of aluminum foil. Let the soap harden. Pull the green soap off the foil. You can rip pieces to look like lettuce.

3 Cut and melt a small amount of the soap. Add fragrance and then the yellow coloring to make cheese. Slowly pour a thin layer of soap onto the aluminum foil. Let the soap harden.

4 Cut a square shape out of the yellow soap with the butter knife to make a piece of cheese. Cut holes out of the cheese with a piece of PVC or a cap from a fragrance container.

5 Prepare the round mold. Cut and melt the soap to make the burger. Add fragrance and brown and red coloring. Pour it into the mold.

6 Prepare the dome-shaped mold. Cut and melt the soap to make the top of the bun. Add a little bit of brown coloring.

7 Use the round mold to make the bottom of the bun.

8 Assemble the burger. Stick the toothpick through it to hold it together. Paint the top bun with some speckles of brown paint if you want.

Pizza Party!

Sure, this soap may not be very useful, but it's a lot of fun to make.

WHAT YOU NEED

Soap: opaque soap base

Molds: plastic stepping-stone mold and a plain-shaped mold

Supplies on page 23

Yellow cornmeal

Yellow, orange, and red coloring

Measuring spoons

Small bowl

Cornstarch

Liquid glycerin*

Cocoa powder

Cheese grater

Blowdryer

* Available at pharmacies and some craft stores

WHAT YOU DO

1 Prepare the stepping-stone mold. Sprinkle some yellow cornmeal into it.

2 Start by making the crust. Cut and melt enough of the soap to fill the mold about ¼ inch. Add a small amount of yellow coloring. Slowly pour the melted soap into the mold. Stop when the crust is about ¼ inch thick.

3 Let the crust cool completely. Unmold it and flip it over so the cornmeal side is facing up. Put it back in the mold.

4 To make the sausage, mix together 4 tablespoons of cornstarch and 4 tablespoons of liquid glycerin. Add cocoa powder until the color looks like sausage. Cut and melt about ½ cup of soap. Pour it into the mixture. Stir the two together until the mixture is cool.

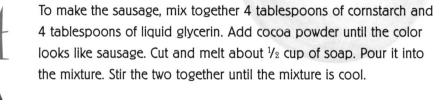

5 Coat your hands with cornstarch and knead the soap. Tear off small, sausage-sized chunks.

6 To make the cheese, prepare the plain-shaped mold. Cut and melt some of the soap. Add some orange coloring, and mix the soap slowly.

7 Pour the soap into the mold. Let it harden. Then unmold it and grate your block of "cheese" into shavings.

8 To make the sauce, melt some more soap base. Add the red coloring. Let the "sauce" cool slightly. Then pour a layer onto the middle of the pizza crust.

9 Immediately place the sausage onto the pizza, then sprinkle the cheese on. Don't completely cover the sausages. Use the blowdryer to melt the cheese on the pizza. Unmold it and cut it into slices for everyone.

Try this!
Have friends make soap in the shape of their favorite pizza toppings. Then you can personalize your slices.

Happy Birthday Cupcakes

These are great favors for a birthday party.

WHAT YOU NEED

Soap: opaque soap base

Mold: muffin tin

Supplies on page 23

Cupcake wrappers

Fragrance of choice

Coloring of choice

Frosting soap*

Bowl

Water

Whisk

Candleholders

Birthday candles

* Available at craft stores

1 Place a cupcake wrapper into each section of the muffin tin.

2 Cut and melt the soap. Add fragrance and coloring. Mix them together slowly.

3 Pour the melted soap into the muffin tin. Let the soap harden.

4 Place the frosting soap in a bowl with some water. (Read the instructions on the soap packaging.) Whisk until the soap triples in size.

5 Frost the cupcakes with the frosting soap.

6 Let the frosting soap set slightly, then place a candleholder and a candle on top of each cupcake.

7 Light the candles and start singing.

Try this!
Make chocolate, strawberry, and vanilla scented cupcakes.

Candy Roll

With a few drops of fragrance, you can make these soaps smell as yummy as they look.

If you want holes in the middle of each soap, take a ¼-inch piece of PVC pipe, center one end of it over the soap, and push down.

 WHAT YOU NEED

Soap: clear soap base
Mold: shallow, round mold
Supplies on page 23
Fragrances for each soap
Colors of choice
Clear plastic wrap
Scissors
Ribbon

 WHAT YOU DO

1 If you have several molds, you can make more than one soap at a time. Prepare the mold(s).

2 Cut and melt the soap. Add the fragrance and coloring for one piece, and mix.

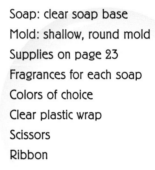

3 Carefully pour the melted soap into the mold. Let the soap harden completely before unmolding. Repeat with the other soaps you've planned to make.

4 Once all the soaps have been unmolded, stack them with a piece of clear plastic between each piece. Then, roll them in plastic wrap, and tie ribbon on both ends.

Eat Your Heart Out

Candy molds are wonderful for making soaps.

 WHAT YOU NEED

Soap: opaque soap base
Mold: heart-shaped candy lollipop mold
Supplies on page 23
Pink coloring
Fragrance of choice
Cosmetic-grade glitter
Lollipop sticks

 WHAT YOU DO

1 Prepare the mold.

2 Cut and melt the soap. Add coloring, fragrance, and glitter. Stir them into the soap slowly.

3 Pour the melted soap into the mold.

4 Place a lollipop stick in each mold. (There should be a special depression in the mold for the stick to go in.) Let the soap harden completely before unmolding.

Ice Treats

Summertime is hot and sticky. Clean up with these cool-as-ice soaps.

 WHAT YOU NEED

Soap: clear soap base
Mold: ice treat tray
Supplies on page 23
Fragrance of choice
Colors of choice
Craft sticks
Rubbing alcohol and sprayer

Did you know that a tribe of people known as the Gauls also discovered soap? But instead of washing with it, they used it to dye their hair red and make it poke out in every direction, hoping to scare off the enemy in battle.

WHAT YOU DO

 1 Prepare the mold. Cut and melt soap for the first layer of the ice treats. Add fragrance and coloring. Mix together slowly.

 2 Pour the soap into the bottom half of each section.

3 When the soap has formed a skin, stick a craft stick into each section.

4 Cut and melt soap for the second layer of the treats. Add fragrance.

5 Let the soap cool slightly so it's no longer steaming.

6 Spritz the first layer with the rubbing alcohol. Pour the next layer on top.

7 Cut and melt the soap for the third layer. Add fragrance and a second color. Mix together slowly. Let the soap cool slightly so it's no longer steaming.

8 Spritz the second layer with the rubbing alcohol. Pour the final layer of soap into the mold. Let it harden completely before umolding.

Crayons

These decorative crayons look great in their wrappers. Simply peel and wash.

WHAT YOU NEED

Soap: clear soap base

Molds: 3-inch length of PVC pipe, ¾ inch in diameter

Supplies on page 23

Polymer clay

Fragrance of choice

Colors of choice

Vegetable peeler

Scissors

Construction paper

Glue stick

 WHAT YOU DO

1 Plug one end of the PVC tube with the polymer clay.

2 Cut and melt the soap for the first crayon. Add fragrance and coloring. Stir them into the soap slowly.

3 Pour the soap into the PVC mold. If the soap's leaking through the bottom, add more polymer clay. Let the soap harden completely.

4 Unmold the soap by pressing on one end with your thumb. Set the soap aside.

5 Repeat steps 1 through 4 for the rest of the crayon soaps you'd like to make.

6 Use the vegetable peeler to shave a point on one end of each of the crayons.

7 When all the soap crayons have set, cut pieces of construction paper to cover them. Wrap the paper around the soap and glue in place.

Your crayons will work best if you use dark colors. Don't be afraid to add a few extra drops of coloring.

 Moldable Soap

Take these soaps into the tub with you and pretend you're Michelangelo.

 WHAT YOU NEED

Soap: opaque soap base

Supplies on page 23

Small glass bowl

1½ tablespoons liquid glycerin*

1 heaping tablespoon cornstarch, plus more for sprinkling

Fragrance of choice

Coloring of choice

* Available at pharmacies and some craft stores

 WHAT YOU DO

1 In the small glass bowl, mix together the liquid glycerin, cornstarch, and fragrance.

2 Sprinkle a sheet of wax paper with some more cornstarch. Set it aside.

3 Cut and melt the soap. Add coloring and stir. Pour it into the glass bowl.

4 Stir the melted soap into the cornstarch mixture. When the soap starts to harden, pick it up and place it on the sheet of wax paper.

5 Coat your hands with cornstarch and knead the soap until it's smooth.

6 Mold and remold the soap into the shapes you want.

Building Blocks

Make 'em. Stack 'em. Use 'em.

 WHAT YOU NEED

Soap: clear soap base

Molds: 2 massage bar molds*

Supplies on page 23

Fragrance of choice

Colors of choice

* These molds have raised (embossed) balls on the bottom.

 WHAT YOU DO

1. Prepare one of the molds. Flip the second soap mold upside down and prepare the outside of that mold.

2. Cut and melt the soap. Add fragrance and coloring. Stir them into the soap slowly. Pour the melted soap into the first mold.

3. As the soap cools, but before it hardens, gently place the second mold on top of the cooling soap so that the massage balls are immersed in the soap. This mold will make the holes in the underside of the bar. Use unused soap blocks to steady the mold on top of the soap.

4. Let the soap harden completely before removing the top mold. Then unmold the soap. Make several more bars so that you can stack them together and build neat stuff with them.

Hanging by a Thread

Hang these soaps from the faucet knobs in your shower.

WHAT YOU NEED

Soap: clear and/or opaque soap base

Molds: all sizes and shapes will work for this project

Supplies on page 23

Fragrance of choice

Coloring of choice

Wooden skewer

Ribbon

WHAT YOU DO

1 Prepare the first mold. Cut and melt the soap for it. Add fragrance and coloring. Stir them into the soap slowly.

2 Pour the melted soap into the mold. Let it harden. Unmold the soap.

3 Repeat steps 1 through 4 until you have made enough soaps.

4 Pierce each piece of soap from one edge to the other with the wooden skewer. Make sure the way you put the hole in is the way you want the soap to hang.

5 Fold the ribbon in half. Put the point of skewer on the fold and push it through the soap. Knot at each end and between each soap.

Rub 'N' Scrub

WHAT YOU NEED

Soap: clear soap base
Mold: deep, clear mold
Supplies on page 23
Bath scrubby with a rope handle
Masking tape
Fragrance of choice
Coloring of choice

It's soap! It's a scrubby!
This two-in-one soap is fun
to use and easy to make.

WHAT YOU DO

1 Prepare the mold. Push the scrubby into the mold until it's all the way inside (except for the string handle).

2 While holding the scrubby down, crisscross strips of masking tape on top of the mold opening. You want the scrubby to be held down securely, but don't cover the whole opening with tape. (You still need space for pouring the soap.)

3 Cut and melt the soap. Add fragrance and coloring. Mix them with the soap slowly.

4 Pour the melted soap slowly into the opening of the mold. Give it some time to seep down through the scrubby. Look through the bottom of the mold to make sure the soap is getting through and surrounding the scrubby. (This is why it's important to use a see-through mold.)

5 Let the soap cool and harden completely. Peel the tape off the top, and pull the soap out by the rope handle.

When your Rub 'N' Scrub runs out of soap, make another one with the same scrubby.

89

Soap on a Rope

The ingredients in this soap are great for really dirty hands and stinky feet.

WHAT YOU NEED

Soap: olive oil or clear soap base

Mold: large tube mold and small tube mold or PVC pipe

Supplies on page 23

Ground oatmeal

Ground cornmeal

Ground coffee

Coffee grinder or food processor (optional)

Aluminum foil

Rubber bands

Polymer clay

Vegetable oil spray or olive oil

Sturdy rope

Wire (optional)

WHAT YOU DO

1 If the oatmeal, cornmeal, and coffee are not already ground, use a coffee grinder or food processor to prepare them. Have an adult help you toast the oatmeal.

2 Wrap aluminum foil around the bottom of the large tube mold, and secure it in place with rubber bands. Make sure to wrap it very tightly so the soap won't seep out of the bottom.

3 Make a plug with the polymer clay that fits the bottom of the small tube mold. Spray the outside of the small tube mold with vegetable spray, then insert it into the larger mold.

4 Cut and melt the soap base. Mix in the oatmeal, cornmeal, and coffee. Stir them very slowly to suspend the ingredients and avoid bubbles.

5 Pour the mixture into the large tube mold. Let the soap cool for about 30 minutes. Remove the outer mold, then the inner one.

6 Slide the rope through the hole and wrap the ends together with wire (or tie a big knot).

91

Vroooom!

The interesting thing about this soap is figuring out how to use it.

WHAT YOU NEED

Soap: clear and opaque soap base
Mold: cookie sheet
Supplies on page 23
Aluminum foil
Fragrance of choice

Black and green coloring
Butter knife
Rubbing alcohol and sprayer
Plastic racing cars

1 Line the cookie sheet with the aluminum foil. Cut and melt a small amount of the opaque soap. Add fragrance and color the soap black. Stir the soap slowly.

2 Pour the melted soap onto the cookie sheet. Let it harden.

3 Take the soap off the cookie sheet. Cut it into a racetrack shape with the butter knife.

4 Line the cookie sheet with aluminum foil again. Set the racetrack on it.

5 Cut and melt the clear soap. Add fragrance, and color the soap light green. Stir it slowly.

6 Spray the racetrack with the rubbing alcohol. Carefully pour the green soap into the cookie sheet. Pour it around and on top of the racetrack.

7 Set the plastic racing cars onto the green layer of soap around the racetrack.

8 Let the soap harden completely. Then take it out of the cookie sheet, and figure out how to use it.

FUN WITH FRIENDS

Get your friends hooked on soapmaking with these fun projects.

Sculpted Masterpieces

This is a cool project to do with a couple of friends. It's fun to see what everyone ends up carving.

 WHAT YOU NEED

Soap: opaque soap base

Mold: rectangular loaf mold

Supplies on page 23

Fragrance of choice

Pencil

Soap carving tools: butter knife, paring knife, and/or vegetable peeler

Soap paints

Paintbrushes

Did you know that many sculptors practice carving first using soap?

 WHAT YOU DO

1 Prepare the mold. Cut and melt the soap. Add fragrance if you want, and stir it into the soap slowly.

2 Pour the melted soap into the mold. Let it harden completely before unmolding.

3 Invite your friends over.

4 Cut bars out of the soap. Draw or trace the shape you want to carve on the soap.

5 Carefully carve the shape out of the soap. Remove the soap slowly, because you can always carve more, but you can't put the soap back on.

6 When you've carved the shape you want, round the edges. Paint the soap.

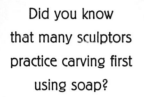

Best Friends

There's only one string attached to this heart!

 WHAT YOU DO

1 Cut the ribbon into a 2- to 3-foot piece, and prepare the mold.

2 Fold the ribbon in half and place both ends in the heart mold. Tape the ribbon in place on the outside of the mold. Make sure the ribbon ends don't touch the mold sides or bottom.

3 Cut and melt the soap base. Add fragrance, coloring, and glitter. Stir them into the soap slowly.

4 Pour the soap into the mold. Let it harden completely.

5 Remove the tape, and take the soap out of the mold. Give your heart away.

MeSSage Soap

Make a statement with this soap, and share it with your friends.

 WHAT YOU NEED

Soap: clear soap base

Mold: any kind you want

Supplies on page 23

Words or image printed on acetate (see instructions on page 31)

Scissors

Rubbing alcohol and sprayer

Fragrance of choice

Coloring of choice

Cosmetic-grade glitter

 WHAT YOU DO

1 Prepare the mold. Cut out the words or image, leaving a ¼-inch margin around the edge. Set it aside.

2 Cut and melt a little bit of the soap. Pour it into the mold so that the melted soap just covers the bottom. Let it set until a skin forms.

3 Spray the acetate with the rubbing alcohol. Place it face down in the soap mold.

4 Cut and melt the rest of the soap. Add the fragrance, coloring, and glitter. Pour the soap into the mold, and let it harden before unmolding.

Slumber Party Pie

Need something to do at your next sleepover? Make this pie soap together, cut it up, and share the slices.

 WHAT YOU NEED

Soap: clear soap base

Mold: large plastic lid from a takeout container

Supplies on page 23

Fragrance of choice

Colors of choice

Rubbing alcohol and sprayer

 WHAT YOU DO

1 Prepare the mold. Cut and melt soap for the first layer. Add fragrance and coloring. Mix the soap slowly.

2 Pour the soap into the mold. Cut and melt soap for the second layer. Add fragrance and coloring. Mix the soap slowly. Let it cool slightly.

3 Once a thin skin has formed on the first layer, spray it with the rubbing alcohol. Pour the second layer on top.

4 Repeat steps 4 and 5 until you've filled the mold. Let the soap harden completely. Take the soap out of the mold and cut it into slices.

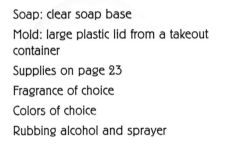

Refer to instructions on pages 28 and 29 for more information on multilayered soaps.

Earth Clay Soap

Clay—it's not at all like putting dirt on your face. These clays clean well, absorb nasty toxins, and won't dry out your skin.

 WHAT YOU NEED

Soap: opaque soap base

Mold: oval mold

Supplies on page 23

1 teaspoon each of powdered red, green, and bentonite clays*

Measuring spoons

Rubbing alcohol and sprayer

* You can find these at most natural food stores.

1 Prepare the mold. Cut and melt enough soap for the first layer. Add the powdered red clay. Stir it into the soap slowly.

2 Pour the melted soap into the mold.

3 Cut and melt soap for the second layer. Add the powdered green clay and mix it into the soap slowly.

4 Let the melted soap cool so that it is no longer steaming. Spray the rubbing alcohol on the first layer of soap once a skin has formed. The skin should be thick enough to hold the weight of the second layer. You can press down with your finger to check.

5 Pour the melted soap into the mold. Let the soap harden.

6 Cut and melt soap for the final layer. Add the powdered bentonite clay and mix it into the soap slowly.

7 Let the melted soap cool slightly. Spray the rubbing alcohol on the second layer of soap.

8 Pour the melted soap into the mold. Let the soap harden completely before unmolding.

101

citrus Loofah

Loofah is a sponge made from the fruit of the loofah plant. (It's a gourd.) It's an awesome exfoliant that removes dead cells from your skin.

 WHAT YOU NEED

Soap: clear soap base
Supplies on page 23
Loofah sponge
Plastic cling wrap
Rubber bands
Orange, lemon, and lime fragrances
Yellow, orange, and green coloring

WHAT YOU DO

1 Cut the loofah sponge into 4-inch-thick pieces.

2 Wrap one end of each loofah piece with plastic cling wrap and secure it in place with several rubber bands. The cling wrap must be very tightly attached to keep the soap from leaking out of the bottom.

3 Cut and melt the soap base. Add fragrance and coloring. Stir the soap slowly.

4 Let the melted base cool slightly, then pour it into the holes in the loofah.

5 After the soap has hardened, remove the plastic cling wrap.

When you cut the end off the loofah, you'll be left with a solid, circular sponge. Place the sponge in a round mold, and then pour the remaining soap base over it. You'll get a sponge coated in soap.

Layered Herb Loaf

Herbs add color, fragrance, and cleansing properties to your soap.

1. Prepare the mold. Cut and melt the soap. Add a handful of dried lavender and stir it in slowly.

2. Pour a thin layer of the mixture into the mold, and let a skin form on the top.

3. Cut and melt more soap. Add a handful of dried rosemary and stir it in slowly.

4. Spray rubbing alcohol on the setting layer of soap.

5. Pour a thin layer of the mixture into the mold, and let a skin form.

6. Cut and melt more soap. Add the dried calendula flower and stir it in slowly.

7. Spray rubbing alcohol on the hardened layer of soap.

8. Pour the mixture into the mold, stopping just short of the lip. Let the final layer cool and harden.

9. Take the soap out of the mold, and slice it into bars.

An Extra-Good Bar of Soap

Sure, all soap gets you clean, but you can make your soap extra special by adding elements that do more than just clean. You can make your soap soothe, moisturize, exfoliate, or just about anything else! Check out this list full of goodies you can add to your soap.

Almond	Moisturizes; soothes; exfoliates
Aloe vera	Moisturizes; heals skin
Calendula	Soothes; softens; heals skin
Chamomile	Soothes; softens; heals skin
Cocoa butter	Moisturizes
Cornmeal	Exfoliates
Eucalyptus	Fragrant; good for muscle aches
Goat's milk	Moisturizes
Green tea	Mild astringent
Ground coffee	Exfoliates
Honey	Moisturizes
Jojoba	Moisturizes
Kelp	Mild astringent
Lady's-mantle	Heals, good for dry skin
Lavender	Stimulates; adds fragrance; healing qualities and a gentle skin cleanser for all skin types
Lemon balm	Soothing; cleanses gently; fragrant
Lovage	Deodorizes
Oatmeal	Exfoliates
Olive oil	Moisturizes
Rose	Refining and hydrating; fragrant
Rosemary	Stimulates; invigorates; good for oily skin; boosts circulation
Seaweed	Mild astringent
Shea butter	Moisturizes
Sweet almond oil	Moisturizes
Tea tree oil	Mild astringent
Valerian	Soothes nerves
Vitamin E	Moisturizes

Lemongrass Soap

This soap may look a little funny,
but it's great for your skin.

WHAT YOU NEED

Soap: clear soap base
Mold: any mold you want
Supplies on page 23
Dried lemongrass
3 tablespoons of liquid aloe

WHAT YOU DO

1 Prepare the mold. Cut and melt the soap. Add a handful of the dried lemongrass and the aloe. Stir them into the soap slowly.

2 Pour the melted soap into the mold. Let it harden completely before unmolding.

Beauty Bar

WHAT YOU NEED

Soap: opaque soap base
Mold: any embossed mold
Supplies on page 23
Beeswax
Shea butter
Measuring spoons
Coloring of choice
Rubbing alcohol and sprayer

This soap is perfect for dry skin.
Shea butter is a rich, creamy moisturizer.

WHAT YOU DO

1 Prepare the mold. Cut and melt the soap. Pour a little into the embossed part of the mold.

2 Cut the beeswax up, and add it to the remaining soap. Then add a tablespoon or more of shea butter. Stir them into the soap. Then add coloring. Mix it all together slowly.

3 Once the first layer of soap has a skin on it, spritz it with the rubbing alcohol.

4 Pour the soap into the mold. Let it harden completely before unmolding.

107

Start Your Own Soap Business

BY BRITTANY JENCKS,
president of Silly Soapers Company, age 12

HOW I GOT STARTED

When I was eight years old, I received a soap kit as a gift. I didn't really do anything with it until I was nine. Then our local homeschooling group had a carnival where kids could sell their handmade crafts. I wanted to sell something, and I asked my parents for help. My mom thought of my soap kit. With the help of my parents, I made a small batch of soap.

Before the carnival, we went to a Chinese restaurant for dinner. The waiter asked about my basket of soap. Before I knew it, I was being invited into the kitchen to show the chef my soap. I sold more soap in that restaurant than I did at the carnival. I enjoyed having my own money and being able to sell things for myself, so I decided to make soap my business.

The first thing I did was build a website. My site was divided in sections using the soap shapes as guides: so I had flying things, swimming things, etc.

CHALLENGES

It took me a while to learn to make good soaps. In the beginning, I added honey, essential oils, herbs, shea butter, coconut, and more! My soaps weren't very colorful, but they smelled good, felt nice on your hands, and were very natural. It didn't take me long to learn that I sell more than twice the soap when I only add colorant and scent. In fact, my most popular soaps are the ones that are the most colorful, attractive, and sweet-smelling.

Another challenge was finding a good way to wrap my soap. At the carnival, I had stuck my soaps in plastic zip-top bags. Not very professional. I just didn't know what to do until, one day, I went to the craft store and bought a roll of something called shrink wrap. My dad wrapped one of my soaps in the shrink wrap and secured the back with a packing label. (Now I secure the wrap on the bottom of the soap with a sticker with my business name on it.) Then he turned on our hairdryer and the plastic shrunk tight around my soap, displaying it clearly and keeping the moisture out. Make sure you don't point the dryer at one place for too long.

As I started getting orders on my website, one problem was that I kept getting custom orders. I would offer, for example, a blue dolphin soap with a rose scent and someone would want a purple one with violet scent. And, believe it or not, I've had some offers from individuals and businesses who wanted really large orders (anywhere from 400 soaps to 4,000!), but I find that I enjoy making soap the most when I can be creative with it and do my own thing. Four thousand bars of one soap would get pretty boring to make and is really something a factory could do just as well.

These are just a few of the soaps I sell. I'm always trying to think of new designs.

FINDING SUCCESS

I've never advertised much. I have business cards, and I've put banners up on websites. I've found that the best advertisement is having my soap in popular stores. I go into the store and tell them a little bit about my soap and business. Then I ask them if they want to carry my soap. Sometimes they give me the business card of the owner, manager, or buyer, and tell me to come back another time. Or sometimes the buyer is there and buys some soap to see how it sells. Sometimes, though, my soap "isn't right" for the store. My best account is with a little toy shop called Once Upon a Time. They buy 6 to 12 soaps every week and they are very nice.

FAVORITE SOAPS TO MAKE

Loaf soap is one of my favorite kinds to make. I chop translucent colored soap into different sizes, spray them with rubbing alcohol, drop them into the mold, and pour in opaque soap. It makes a really cool kaleidoscope effect when I slice it into bars.

Another easy but impressive-looking soap is using layers. I have a few molds with angels on them. I like to pour the wings gold or a translucent white and the rest of the bar another color.

OTHER ADVICE

• Take care of your supplies, and buy them wholesale in large quantities. The Internet is a good place to shop. Buying soap in two-pound bricks at the craft store is extremely expensive if you are making a lot of soap.

• Don't give up. It takes time to get a successful business started. It took me three years to get my account with Once Upon a Time.

• Don't get discouraged by mean or grumpy people.

• Above all...have fun.

Troubleshooting

Even though soapmaking is easy, you might run into some occasional difficulties, especially when you're just starting out. The following is a list of common situations that happen to most soapmakers at one time or another and some possible explanations and solutions.

Problem
Difficulty unmolding soap

Explanation and Solution
Your soap may not be cool and hard yet. Wait a few minutes longer. The next time you use the same mold, use a mold release, such as vegetable oil spray or petroleum jelly.

Problem
Bubbles in finished soap

Explanation and Solution
Stir your soap gently—vigorous stirring creates bubbles that are difficult to remove. Before your soap starts to cool, spray the surface of your soap with alcohol to remove bubbles that may have formed.

Problem
Cracking, breaking soap

Explanation and Solution

Cracks are caused by lack of moisture. Your soap could have lost moisture through overheating or by being placed in the freezer. You can remelt the soap, then add a little more soap base to regain some of the lost moisture.

Problem
Embedded soap is melting

Explanation and Solution
The soap that you poured over the embeds was too hot. Wait a few moments for the soap to cool slightly before adding melted base on top of soap embeds.

Another problem might be that the embedded soap was sliced too thin. An embedded soap should be at least $\frac{1}{8}$ inch thick to protect it from melting.

Problem
Sweating soap (that is, beads of moisture have accumulated on the surface, creating an unattractive appearance)

Explanation and Solution
Unwrapped soaps will often attract moisture, especially in areas where there's a lot of humidity in the air. Make sure to wrap your soap as soon as it has cooled and hardened. This problem may also happen when you use poor-quality soap base. If the problem continues after you've wrapped the soaps, try a different soap base.

Problem
Scent disappears

Explanation and Solution
You may not be working with a cosmetic-grade fragrance. Your soap base could also be low quality, or you may have overheated the soap and caused the fragrance to burn off. Add an extra couple of drops next time or try a different soap base.

Problem
Splits in layered soap

Explanation and Solution
Spray the first layer with alcohol before pouring on a second layer—this helps the layers stick. Also, your first layer should still be slightly warm (but firm enough to support another layer) when the second is poured.

Problem
Bleeding colors

Explanation and Solution
This problem can happen when you use a poor-quality colorant (such as food coloring). Make sure you use coloring that's made for soap.

Problem
Cloudy soap

Explanation and Solution
You probably overheated the soap. Always keep an eye on your melting soap. Don't let the soap bubble in the microwave.

Problem
Your mold warped

Explanation and Solution
Your soap was too hot. Let your soap base cool for 5 minutes before pouring it in the mold next time.

Metric Conversion Chart

¼ inch = 6 mm
½ inch = 1.3 cm
¾ inch = 1.9 cm
1 inch = 2.5 cm
1½ inches = 3.8 cm
2 inches = 5.1 cm
2½ inches = 6.4 cm
3 inches = 7.6 cm
3½ inches = 8.9 cm
4 inches = 10.2 cm
4½ inches = 11.4 cm
5 inches = 12.7 cm

To convert inches to centimeters, multiply by 2.5.
To convert ounces to grams, multiply by 28.
To convert teaspoons to milliliters, multiply by 5.
To convert tablespoons to milliliters, multiply by 15.
To convert fluid ounces to milliliters, multiply by 30.
To convert cups to liters, multipy by .24.
To convert degrees Fahrenheit to degrees Celsius, subtract 32 and then multiply by .56.

Index

The End